Sukhmani Sahib Englisl

Copyright 2014

ISBN-13: 978-1500307547

ISBN-10: 1500307548

Foreword

The word **Sukhmani**, when given an English meaning, can translate into several versions. Some of the commonly preferred titles are, *'Gem of Peace'*, *'Jewel of Peace'*, *'Song of Peace'* and *'Psalm of Peace'*.

Appearing on page 262 to page 296 of the *Sri Guru Granth Sahib*, the Sikh Holy Scriptures, it is a set of hymns divided into 24 sections. Each section consists of 8 hymns, known as *Astpadi*. Every hymn is preceded by a verse, known as *Salok*.

So the format will start with a verse (*Salok*), followed by 8 hymns (*Astpadi*), which make up one section. The whole prayer comprises of 24 sections, just like 24 hours comprise a day.

The fifth Sikh Guru, Guru Arjan Dev Ji, compiled this set of 192 Hymns. His Holiness, *Guru Arjan Dev Ji*, never uses his name even once in the composition, opting instead to use the name *Nanak*, to refer and honor the first and founding Sikh Guru, **Guru Nanak Dev Ji**.

I have used the word *'Name'* in place of the *Gurmukhi* word *'Naam'* for your easy understanding. Both denote the same meaning, which is *'The Name of God'*.

This book is only possible by divine inspiration and the Almighty's grace. The goal of this book is to give readers who don't understand *Gurmukhi* (the language in which the scriptures were written), a chance to understand how magnificent this lengthy composition is. It takes about 60 to 90 minutes to recite the whole prayer.

I will present a brief synopsis of the message each section intends to convey. Then I will present the entire 192 hymns. Please keep in mind that it is my humble attempt to explain the message of the divine, and I'm sure it will reveal more interesting and different angles to the reader once they have read it. Don't be surprised if every reading reveals something new.

I wish the reader Happiness and may you attain peace of mind after reading this divine composition, and imbibe its teachings into your everyday life.

THANK YOU GOD

Brief Synopsis of the 24 sections (*Astpadis*)

1. Sums up the benefits of meditation and contemplating on the Lord.
2. Tells us that by being pious and practicing Holiness, we reduce our ability to sin.
3. The Guru tells us that performing austerities or studying holy texts etc, cannot compare to reading or listening to the sacred Word of the Lord.
4. Emphasizes the need for good morals and behavior.
5. Teaches us gratitude and to thank God for all his gifts and blessings to us.
6. Tells us of the different types of gifts and blessings that the Lord has bestowed on us.
7. Discusses the attributes and characteristics of the Saints.
8. Carries from the 7th section, it glorifies the virtues of the God-oriented man, the Brahm-giani.
9. *Guru Arjan Dev* defines the various types of Holy Persons.
10. This section deals with the various types of people and substances, both good and bad.
11. Tells us that the humble and meek win God's Love, while the vain and egoistic one find no peace or joy.
12. This section dwells on the people that are arrogant and boastful.
13. Teaches us of the need to associate with the Saints and refrain from slandering them.

14. Points to us that mortals cannot be relied on. They are volatile and unreliable.
15. Tells us that just as darkness is dispelled by light, the Guru's teachings and instructions awakens the mind.
16. The Guru points to us that the Supreme God is the Playwright, Director and Actor in his own plays.
17. Here, the Guru emphasizes the unique qualities of a true servant of God, namely humility and obedience.
18. This section stresses the characteristics of a true seeker of truth.
19. Guru Ji warns us of the various distractions of life, such as amassing wealth and all impermanent things that we have to leave behind when we depart.
20. This section tells us of the efforts we need to put for spiritual progress.
21. Guru Ji tells us of the void that prevailed before the Lord created the World.
22. While God's attributes are infinite, His Holiness points out a few, namely generosity and goodness.
23. Reveals to us the omnipotence of God, who created the expanse of the Universe.
24. The final section tells us of the benefits of Sukhmani. The true devotee will be blessed with positive attributes, namely health, wisdom and everlasting peace.

With the Lord's grace and blessings, I humbly present you the Holy Sukhmani Sahib in English.

Begins with Salutation by Guru Arjan Dev Ji to the Supreme Lord, followed by the hymns.

One Universal Creator God. Attained by the grace of the True Guru.

Salok 1
I bow to God, who is the Creator of all.
I bow to God, who existed even before the ages began.
I bow to God, the True One.
I bow to the Great, Divine God.

Astpadi (Verse) 1

Meditate, Meditate in remembrance of Him, and obtain peace.
Worry and Anguish shall be dispelled from you.
Remember and praise the One who pervades the whole Universe.
Countless people, in various ways, chant his Name.
The Vedas, Puranaas and Simritees (Ancient Holy Scriptures),
Were created from the One Word, the Name of the Lord.
That person, in whose heart and soul the One Lord dwells,
Praises of such a person, cannot be recounted.
Those devotees who yearn for the blessing to have one glance of
You,
O Lord, keep me in the company of such a person, and save me
along with them. [1]

Sukhmani: Peace of Mind; the Nectar of the Name of God.
The minds of the devotees abide in a joyful peace.
Remembering God, one does not have to enter in the womb of
reincarnation again.
Remembering God, the fear of Death is dispelled.
Remembering God, Death keeps a distance,
Remembering God, one's enemies (the five evil vices – Lust, Anger,
Greed, Attachment, Pride) retreat.
Remembering God, no obstacles are met.
Remembering God, one remains aware and alert, night and day.
Remembering God, one is not touched by fear.
Remembering God, one does not suffer.
The remembrance of God is obtained in the society of the true
devotees.
O Nanak, all treasures and wealth are obtained by sincere devotion
and Love for God. [2]

By remembering God, one obtains spiritual and supernatural powers
and the nine treasures.
By remembering God, one obtains divine knowledge, meditation and
the essence of wisdom.
Remembrance of God, is the true form of penances, devotion and
worship.
In the remembrance of God, duality is removed.

4

By remembering God, one takes purifying baths at sacred shrines and places of pilgrimage.
By remembering God, one attains the honor in the Court of the Lord.
In the remembrance of God, one becomes a good person.
By remembering God, one reaps the true fruit (true purpose of human life.
They alone remember Him in meditation, whom he inspires and blesses to meditate.
Nanak touches the feet of such humble beings. [3]

The remembrance of God is the highest and most exalted of all.
In the remembrance of God, many are saved.
In the remembrance of God, thirst (yearning and desires) are quenched.
By remembering Him, all things are known (what is good, what is bad).
By remembering God, the fear of Death is removed.
By remembering God, all hopes and desires are fulfilled (the devotee does not yearn anymore).
By remembering God, the filth of the mind is washed off,
And the Name of the Lord is absorbed into one's heart.
God abides on the tongues of His Saints.
Nanak wants to become the slave of slaves, of such true Saints. [4]

Those who remember God are wealthy (in the true sense).
Those who remember God are honorable.
Those who remember God are welcome and accepted (both in the world and after death).
Those who remember God are the most distinguished persons.
Those who remember God, depend on none and are not lacking.
Those who remember God are the true rulers of all.
Those who remember God, dwell in peace.
Those who remembering God live forever (free from bondage of birth and death).
Only those, upon whom he showers his grace, get to truly remember him.
Nanak prays (and tells us to pray) for the dust of the feet of such Saints. [5]

Those who remember God are generous and help others.

I am forever a sacrifice to those, who remember God.
Those who remember God – their faces are glowing.
Those who remember God abide in peace.
Those who remember God, conquer their souls (mind).
Those who remember God have a pure, moral and spotless lifestyle.
Those who remember God, experience all forms of joy.
Those who remember God, dwell close to the Lord.
They remain awake and watchful (attached to God) night and day,
by the grace of the Saints.
O Nanak, this gift of meditative remembrance of God only comes by
perfect destiny. [6]

By remembering God, everything gets accomplished.
Remembering God, one never grieves.
By remembering God, one utters his praises.
Remembering God, one is easily absorbed into a meditative state.
Remembering God, one attains the unchanging position (everlasting
place in God's Kingdom).
Remembering God, one's heart's blooms like a lotus.
Remembering God, the unstruck melody vibrates.
The Peace and Joy, which are attained by remembering him, have no
end or limits.
They alone remember him, upon whom God bestows his Grace.
Nanak seeks the sanctuary of those humble beings. [7]

By remembering God, his Saints get distinction and fame.
Remembering the Lord, the Vedas were composed.
Remembering God, men obtain supernatural powers, remain content
and give to others.
Remembering the Lord, the lowly become known in all four
directions.
The remembrance of God supports the whole World.
Remember, remember in meditation the Lord, the Creator, the cause
of causes.
For the remembrance of the Lord, He created the whole world.
Where God is remembered, he is present there.
By His grace, He himself imparts this understanding.
To such sincere devotees, God gives the boon of remembering His
Name, though the true Guru, says Nanak. [8]   (1)

Salok 2

O Destroyer of the pain and grief of the distressed,
O Master of each and every Heart, the Helper of the Helpless...
O Master-less One,
I have come seeking your Sanctuary,
O Lord, please be with Nanak.

Astpadi (Verse) 2

Where there is no Mother, Father, Children, Friends or Siblings,
O My Mind, there, only the name of the Lord, shall be with you as
your help and support.
Where the great and terrible Messenger of Death await to crush you,
There, only the Name of the Lord shall protect you.
Where there are great obstacles in your path,
There the Name of God shall protect and rescue you.
By performing countless religious rituals, you shall not be saved.
The Name of the Lord washes off millions of sins.
As *Gurmukh* (follower of Guru), chant the Name of the Lord, O my
mind.
O Nanak, you shall obtain countless joy. [1]

Even if one becomes the Ruler of the entire World, he is still
unhappy and miserable.
By chanting the Name of the Lord, one becomes Happy.
Even if you were to acquire millions upon millions, your desires still
will not be contained.
By chanting the Name of the Lord, your desires can be quelled.
With the countless pleasures of Maya, your thirst shall not be
quenched.
Chanting the Name of the Lord, you shall be satisfied.
The road on which you have to travel alone (after death, or even
while alive),
There, only the Lord's Name will accompany and sustain you.
On such a Name, O my mind, meditate continuously forever.
O Nanak, as a *Gurmukh* (follower of Guru) you shall obtain the state
of supreme dignity. [2]

Even though the man may have millions of arms (friends and family), still he shall not be saved.
But by chanting the Name with devotion, he shall swim across (the worldly ocean).
When countless misfortunes threaten to destroy you,
The Name of the Lord shall protect and rescue you.
Through countless incarnations, people are born and die, come and go.
Chanting the Name of the Lord, you shall finally come to rest in peace (union with God).
The ego is polluted with filth, which can never be washed off.
But the Name of God washes away millions of Sins.
O my Mind, continuously chant such a Name with Love and devotion.
O Nanak, it is obtained in the company of the Holy. [3]

On that path where the miles can never be counted,
There, the Name of the Lord shall be your sustenance.
On that journey in total pitch darkness,
The Name of the Lord shall accompany you and give you light.
On that journey where no one knows you,
With the Name of the Lord, you shall be recognized.
On that path, there is terrible and unbearable heat,
There, the Name of the Lord will give you shade.
O my mind, where thirst torments you to cry out,
There, O Nanak, the Name of the Lord shall rain nectar upon you.
[4]

The Name is the indispensable necessity for the true Saint,
The Name resides within the Saints heart.
The Name of God is the shelter of His servants,
Millions have been saved by God's Name.
Day and night, saints praise God.
They store the Name of God as their medicine (for removing all evil).
The Name of God is the treasure of the holy man.
The Supreme Being bestows the gift of the Name on his devotees.

Their bodies and souls are dyed with the love of the One God.
Nanak (Guru), the saints get the divine knowledge and power of distinguishing between evil and virtue. -5-

The Name of God is the way, by which His devotees attain salvation.
The Name of God satiates all the hungers of his devotees.
The Name of God is the beauty and joy of His servants.
By uttering God's Name, no harm or obstacles come.
The Name of God is the honor and glory of His devotees.
He (His devotees) obtains fame through the God's Name.
The Name of God is the true form of meditation.
By uttering His Name, he never suffers any pain and separation from God.
God's devotees always remain attached in the service (repetition) of His Name.
Nanak (Guru says), that the true Saints worship only One God. -6-

The Name of God is the true wealth and treasure for his devotees,
The wealth of God's Name is conferred by God Himself to his devotees.
God's Name is the powerful stronghold of His devotees.
God's devotees do not need any other support.
God's devotee is thoroughly dyed with God's Love,
By repeating God's Name, his mind reaches the state of meditation, where no worldly thought disturbs him.
The devotees of God repeat His Name throughout the day.
Such a Saint gains distinction and cannot remain unnoticed.
The worship of God confers salvation on many.
Nanak (Guru says), many more swim across the worldly ocean by joining the company of such saints. -7-

The Name of God is the miraculous tree (which fulfills all desires),
The singing of God's praises possesses the power of the 'Kamdheen' cow(mythical cow that fulfills all desires).
The singing of God's praises is the best of all (religious) discourses.
On hearing the Name, pain and sorrow vanish.
The divine virtues of the Name reside within the saint's heart.
By the kindness of the saint, sins depart.

Association with the saints is obtained through gross luck and Destiny.
It is by serving them that one meditates on God's Name.
There is nothing equal to the Name.
Nanak(Guru says), a few obtain(the gift of) the Name by following the instructions of the Guru. -8- (2)

Salok 3

I have seen many *Shastras* (scriptures) and *Simitis*
And have searched them all;
But they are not equal to the priceless Name of God,
Nanak(Guru says).

Astpadi (Verse) 3

Uttering spells, practicing penances, pretending to possess knowledge and meditating,
The exposition of the holy scriptures,
The practice of Yoga, practice of religious ceremonies
The abandonment of all and wandering in the forests;
Different types of efforts;
Alms giving, sacrifice, and burning of eatables in fire,
Cutting one's body into pieces and offering them to the fire,
Observing fasts and taking vows of many kinds,
(All of the above acts) are not equal to the contemplation and worship of the Name of God.
Nothing compares to the sincere repetition of God's Name, be it even once. -1-

If one were to wander through the nine continents of the earth, and were to live a long life;
If one were to become a great pious person,
If one were to burn oneself in the fire of ego,
If one were to make gifts of gold, horses and land,
If one were to perform supernatural feats,

If one were to adopt mortification, as practiced by Jains, and were to make great spiritual efforts;
If one were to cut one's body into pieces;
Even then, the filth of pride would not depart.
All these efforts are not equal to the Name if God.
Nanak (Guru says), by repeating the Name, the true devotee obtains salvation. -2-

Even though man may wish that his soul should leave his body at a place of pilgrimage,
Even then, pride and arrogance will not leave the mind.
Even though man may go on taking holy baths throughout his life,
Still the filth of the mind will not be cleaned away.
Even if man were to subject his body to severe mortifications,
Still the poison of mammon will not abandon the mind.
Even though one may wash his perishable body with lots of water,
Yet how can this wall of mud(body) be cleansed?
O my soul, the glory of the Name of God is much exalted.
Nanak (Guru says), with the help if the Name, countless sinners have been saved. -3-

Despite man's cleverness the fear of death will overpower him.
Even by various efforts, the thirst will not be quenched.
Even by adopting various religious grabs, the fire of the worldly love will not be put off.
Even by adopting millions of such methods, man is still not acceptable in God's court.
He shall still not be liberated reaching the sky or going to the nether regions.
On the contrary he becomes even more entangled in the net of worldly love.
Apart from the Name, all other methods result in punishment by the messenger of death.
The messenger of death does not care for anything except the worship and praises of God.
By repeating the Name of God, pain and grief vanish.
Nanak (Guru), utters the Name without any effort and is unaffected by mammon. -4-

If anyone wants the four boons of faith, wealth, fulfillment of desires

and salvation,
He should engage himself in the service of the Holy men.
If anyone wants freedom from pain and trouble,
He should always sing the Name of God within his heart.
If anyone seeks honor for himself,
He should renounce his pride by joining the society of holy men.
If anyone fears transmigration, He should fall at the feet of the true saints.
To the devotee who is thirsty for the sight of God,
Nanak(Guru), is always a sacrifice to him. -5-

Among all men, he is the foremost,
Whose pride is effaced by joining the society of the true saints.
He, who considers himself to be lowly,
Shall be counted as the most exalted of all.
He, whose mind has no ego,
Shall see God and His Name present in all hearts.
He, who expels evil from his heart,
Shall regard the whole world as his friends.
Such devotees regard pain and pleasure alike,
Nanak(Guru says), they are unaffected by evil and good(they commit no evil). -6-

O God, for him who has no wealth, Your Name is the wealth.
For him who has no home, Your Name is home.
O God, for the one who has no honor, Your Name is their honor.
O God, You give gifts to all.
O God, you act and cause others to act as it pleases you.
Only you know the secrets of all hearts.
O God, You know your own condition, glory and limits.
You are absorbed on your own self.
It is You alone, who can praise yourself.
Nanak (Guru says), none else knows or can fully narrate Your praises. -7-

Of all religions, the best one is,
To sincerely utter the Name of God; and this is the most pious work.
Of all the religious deeds, the best one is,
To remove the filth of evil instincts and inclinations by joining the society of true saints.

Of all efforts, the best one is,
To always repeat the Name of God within one's heart.
Of all speeches, the divine speech is,
To utter with tongue and to hear with ears, the praises of God.
Of all places (pilgrimages etc.), that place (heart) is the best,
Where the Name of God comes to reside, Nanak(Guru says). -8- (3)

Salok 4
O unworthy, innocent, and virtue less man,
Remember in your heart your Creator,
Who will accompany and help you everywhere.

Astpadi (Verse) 4

O man, remember and ponder over the excellences of the great God.
From what origin he made you and how you appear now.
Remember God who made, fashioned and adorned you.
Who preserved you in the fire if the womb,
Who provided milk for you to drink in your infancy.
Who gave you nourishment, comfort and intelligence in your youth.
Who gave you relatives to serve you in your old age,
And who put food in your mouth while you are seated.
The thankless and unworthy man does not value these favors;
Nanak(Guru prays), O God, pardon him so that he may acquire true understanding. -1-

O man, do not forget God by whose favor you live comfortably on the earth;
Make merriments with your children, siblings, friends and spouse.
By whose favor you drink cool water;
And the pleasant winds and priceless fire serve you.
By whose favor you enjoy all pleasures;
And get all the necessities of life.
Do not forget God who gave you hands, feet, ears, eyes and tongue.
Why have you abandoned Him and attached yourselves with others?
Alas, the foolish and blind men are entangled in sins.
Nanak (Guru prays), O God, save them from these sins. -2-

God, Who protects you from birth till death,
The ignorant fool does not love Him.
By serving whom he can attain the nine treasures,
The fool does not attach his mind with Him.
God is ever present,
But the blind man thinks Him to be far away.
By serving Whom, he gets honored in His court,
But the foolish and stupid man forgets Him.
Man ever and forever commits errors;
Nanak(Guru says), the infinite God is the Preserver of all. -3-

Man abandons the Jewel of the Name and is attached to the shell of
mammon.
He renounces the truth and gloats over falsehood.
What he has to leave behind, he thinks it to be permanent.
What will happen (death), he thinks it to be far away.
He works hard to obtain that, which he must leave behind.
And he spurns (God) the Helper, Who resides within him.
He washes away and removes the coating of sandal,
And like a donkey, loves to roll in the ashes.
The sinner has fallen into a terrible blind well;
Nanak(Guru prays), O God, save him. -4-

The sinner is a man only on appearance; but his acts are like those of
a brute.
He cheats others day and night,
He wears religious robes, but within him is present the filth of
worldly love.
However much he may try, he cannot conceal his deeds.
Outwardly, he practices contemplation, meditation and ablution,
While his heart is like a greedy dog.
In his heart exists the fire of greed, while he poses to be a saint by
applying ashes to his body.
There is a stone (loads of sins) tied to his neck;
How can he swim across the world ocean?
He, in whose heart God resides,
Shall be absorbed in Him(God), Nanak(Guru says). -5-

How can a blind man (sinner) find the way only by hearing?
O God, take his hand so he may reach the ultimate goal of life.

How can the deaf man understand riddles?
If you tell him of the night, he will think if the dawn.
How can a dumb man sing a stave?
Even if he attempts, his voice will break.
How can a cripple roam on the mountains?
He can never reach there.
The helpless man should pray to God, the Ocean of Mercy, this:
"I can swim across only by your kindness and mercy", Nanak (Guru says). -6-

God, the Helper, who resides with the man, is not remembered by Him.
He loves that which is his enemy (mammon).
The man lives in the house of sand.
He indulges in joys and pleasures of Maya (mammon).
He is fully confident (under delusion of mammon) in his mind(that he is immortal).
And the thought of death never crosses his mind.
Revenge, enmity, lust, anger and worldly love;
Falsehood, sinful deeds, greed and deceit(are loved by the sinner).
In this way he has passed through several births.
Nanak (Guru prays), O God, save him by your kindness. -7-

O God, You are The Lord. I make this supplication to You.
The soul and body are all your property.
You are (our) Mother and Father and we are all your children.
By your favor we attain many comforts.
None knows your limits.
O God, you are the most exalted of the exalted.
All the creations are strung upon your string (supported by your laws).
Whatever has been created by You, is working under Your orders.
You alone know your condition and limits.
Nanak (Guru says), Your slave is ever a sacrifice to You. -8- (4)

Those who forget God and attach themselves to other pleasures (worldly),
Such ones shall never be successful(acceptable to God),
For without the Name, their honor shall depart, Nanak(Guru says).

Astpadi(Verse) 5

Man obtains ten things (many gifts from God) and lays them aside(without thanking the Giver),
He shall forfeit his faith(by being angry) for the loss of even one thing.
If God were to not give even one thing, and were to take away the ten things also,
Then what can the fool do?
With The Lord, force is of no avail,
Always bow down before him. -1-

The Banker(God) gives the capital(of countless things) to man;
He eats, drinks and uses them with great pleasure and joy.
But if the Banker(God), takes back some out of which He has entrusted to man,
The ignorant fool becomes angry and us aggrieved in his mind.
Thus he forfeits confidence by his own act,
And he shall not be trusted again.
If man place the things before the Owner(God);
And obeys His orders without objections;
God will make him fourfold happy.
Nanak(Guru says), God is ever merciful. -2-

The attachment with worldly things is of various kinds.
Know this for certain, that they are temporary.
The man loves the shadow of the tree(mammon);
When it vanishes, he repents in his heart.
Whatever is seen, is perishable;
Yet the man, who is completely blind(ignorant), remains attached to it.
He, who cherishes love with a traveler,

Shall gain nothing useful.

O my soul, the love for God's Name gives peace and comfort.

Nanak(Guru says), God attaches to Himself those, to whom He shows mercy. -3-

Perishable are body, wealth and the entire family;

Perishable are pride, ego and worldly love;

Perishable are kingdom, youth, wealth and property;

Perishable are lust and anger;

Perishable are chariots, elephants, horses and regiments;

Perishable is the attachment with Maya(worldly things) by be holding which, the man takes pleasure;

Perishable are deceit, worldly love and pride;

Perishable is the self-conceit;

(Only) the worship(of God), performed under the protection of the (true) Guru, is imperishable.

Nanak(Guru says), one can live the true life only by meditating upon God's feet. -4-

Vain are the ears, which listens to the slander of others;

Vain are the hands, which steal the property of others;

Vain are the eyes, which behold the beauty and charm of other women;

Vain is the tongue, which tastes food and delicacies(without remembering God).

Vain are the feet, which run to commit sins;

Vain is the mind, which covets other's wealth.

Vain is the body, which does not work for the benefit of others.

Vain is the nose, which enjoys the smell if evil;

Without understanding(God, and the true purpose of life) one won't realize that everything is perishable.

Nanak(Guru says), the body, which remembers God, is a worthy one. -5-

Useless is the life of the infidel,

How can man become pure without worshipping the True God and His Name?

Useless is the body of the spiritually blind without worship of the Lord's Name.

Foul breath(language) comes from his mouth.

Without remembering the Name, his days and nights pass away in

vain;
Just as the crops perishes without the rain.
Without the worship of God, all deeds are rendered fruitless,
Like the wealth of a miser, which remains useless.
They, in whose heart the Name if God resides, are to be
congratulated.
Nanak(Guru says), I am a sacrifice to them. -6-

He who professes one thing but does something else;
In whose heart there is no true love for God, but who attracts men to
himself by his sweet talk;
God, Who knows everything, is wise;
He cannot be pleased by outer appearances.
He who preaches but does not practice what he preaches,
Shall come and go, take birth and die(over and over again).
There are men in whose hearts the formless one resides;
Through their sermons, the world will be saved.
Only they, who are pleasing to you, O God, can realize you.
Nanak(Guru advises us), to fall at the feet of such men. -7-

Whatever I pray for, the Supreme Being knows all.
God Himself confers honor on His creatures.
God Himself gives judgments according to the good and evil deeds
of men.
He shows Himself afar to some and near to others.
He Himself is free and above all;
He thoroughly knows the ways and spiritual condition if the hearts
of all men.
God attaches the man, who is pleasing to Him, to his helm(makes
him His devotee).
God is present everywhere.
He, to whom He is kind, becomes His attendant.
Nanak(Guru says), remember God every moment. -8- (5)

Salok 6

O God, kindly cause lust, anger, greed, attachment and egoism to depart.
O God, I have taken your protection.
Divine God, please grant(this prayer of Guru) Nanak.

Astpadi(Verse) 6

By whose kindness you eat thirty-six(various) kinds of dishes;
Keep that Lord always on your mind.
By whose kindness you apply perfume on your body;
You shall obtain salvation by remembering Him.
By whose kindness you live comfortably at home;
Meditate on Him continuously in your heart.
By whose kindness you live comfortably with your family,
Repeat His Name with your tongue throughout the eight
watches(twenty four hours).
By whose kindness you enjoy pleasure and merriment,
Ever meditate on Him, Who is worthy of meditation, Nanak(Guru
says). -1-

By whose kindness you wear silk and satin;
Why should you forget Him and attach to others?
By whose kindness you sleep in comfort on your bed;
O my mind, sing His praises throughout the eight watches(twenty
four hours).
By whose kindness you are honored by all,
Repeat His praises with your mouth.
By whose kindness your faith is preserved,
O mind, ever meditate upon the Supreme being alone.
By uttering the Name of God, you shall attain honor on His court.
Nanak(Guru says), you will then go to the real home(heaven) with
honors. -2-

By whose kindness your beautiful body remains healthy,
Meditate on that lovable God.
By whose kindness your evils remain unknown,
O mind, get peace and happiness by uttering His praises.
By whose kindness all your defects get concealed,
O mind, take shelter of that Lord.
By whose kindness none can become your equal,
O mind, with every breath remember the Supreme Lord.
By whose kindness you have obtained this human body,
Worship Him, Nanak(Guru says). -3-

By whose kindness you were ornaments,
O mind, why do you hesitate to remember Him?
By whose kindness you ride on horses and elephant;
O mind, never forget that God.
By whose kindness you are fortunate to possess gardens, property
and wealth;
Keep that God in your heart.
O mind, God who made the frame of your body,
Continue meditating on Him, whether standing or seated.
Meditate upon Him, Who is the invisible and Indescribable One.
And He will preserve your honor in this world and the next,
Nanak(Guru says). -4-

By Whose kindness you give a lot in charity;
Meditate upon Him during the eight watches if the day.
By Whose kindness you perform your religious and worldly duties,
Remember that God with every breath.
By Whose kindness your form is so beautiful,
Ever remember that most beautiful God.
By Whose kindness you obtained the superior status(of a human);
Meditate on that God day and night.
By whose favor your honor is maintained;
Repeat His praises with the grace of the Guru(says Guru), Nanak.-5-

By Whose kindness you hear the melody with your ears,
By Whose kindness you see wonders,
By Whose kindness you utter sweet words with your tongue;
By Whose kindness you live in ease and comfort;

By Whose kindness your hands and body discharge their duties;
By Whose kindness you succeed;
By Whose kindness you obtain the supreme blissful state;
By Whose kindness you obtain Happiness and peace of mind,
Why do you forget such a God and attach yourself to others(mammon)?
Nanak(Guru says), awaken your mind with the grace of the Guru.-6-

By Whose kindness you have become known in the world;
Do not forget at all, that God, in your heart.
By Whose kindness you obtain glory.
O foolish mind, repeat His Name.
By Whose kindness your affairs are accomplished;
Believe in your kind that He is ever-present.
By Whose kindness you obtain the truth;
O my mind, remain attached to Him.
By Whose kindness all are saved;
Nanak(Guru says), utter his Name. -7-

He utters the Name if God, whom He(God) causes to utter.
He sings God's praises, whom He(God) causes to sing.
With the grace of God, the divine knowledge dawns in the mind.
With the grace if the God, the lotus(heart) blooms.
When God is pleased, He resides in the mind.
By God's kindness, man attains true wisdom.
All wealth can be obtained by your grace(O God).
No one can obtain anything by himself(by his own efforts).
O Lord, wherever you appoint us, we apply ourselves to those duties.
Nanak(Guru says), the created ones have nothing(no power) in their hands. -8- (6)

Salok 7
The Supreme being is inaccessible and unfathomable,
Whoever repeats His Name shall be saved.
Listen, O my friend, Nanak(Guru) tells;
The wonderful story of the saints(who have conquered their mind and merged with God).

Astpadi(Verse) 7

By association with saints, the face becomes radiant
By association with saints, the filth of sins is removed.
By association with saints, pride vanishes.
By association with saints, divine knowledge is revealed.
By association with saints, God is felt just nearby.
By association with saints, everything becomes well settled.
By association with saints, the Jewel of The Name us obtained.
By association with saints, man strives to realize One God.
How can the mortal narrate the glory of the saints?
Nanak(Guru says), the glory of the saints merges with the glory of
God. -1-

By association with saints, the Unseen God can be realized.
By association with saints, man ever flourishes.
By association with saints, the five evil passions are subdued.
By association with saints, man tastes the nectar of the Name.
By association with saints, man becomes humble.
By association with saints, one's speech becomes fascinating.
By association with saints, the mind does not wander in any
direction.
By association with saints, the mind becomes stable.
By association with saints, the mind is detached from mammon
By association with saints, God showers His mercy, Nanak(Guru
says). -2-

By association with saints, all enemies become friends.
By association with saints, man becomes very pure.
By association with saints, man feels enmity to no one
By association with saints, one does not sway from the path.
By association with saints, man dies not look at anybody with evil
intent.
By association with saints, man realizes The Lord of Supreme joy.
By association with saints, the malady of pride departs.
By association with saints, man abandons self-conceit.
Only God knows the greatest if saints.
Nanak(Guru says), there is close understanding between God and
His saints. -3-

By association with saints, the mind never wanders.
By association with saints, true joy is obtained.
By association with saints, man receives God's Name.
By association with saints, man bears the unbearable.
By association with saints, man reaches an exalted position.
By association with saints, man reaches the palace(of God).
By association with saints, man realizes the essence of all religions.
By association with saints, man sees the Supreme Being everywhere.
By association with saints, man obtains the treasure of the Name
Nanak(Guru says), I am a sacrifice to the saints. -4-

By association with saints, one's entire family is saved.
By association with saints, friends, relatives and acquaintances are
saved.
By association with saints, true wealth is obtained;
By which everyone gains power and fame.
By association with saints, Dharam Raj(God of justice) serves,
By association with saints, gods and angels sing the praises.
By association with saints, sins depart.
By association with saints, man sings of the nectarine qualities.
By association with saints, man reaches every place(obtains spiritual
powers).
By association with saints, Human birth bears fruit Nanak(Guru
says). -5-

By association with saints, man need not perform painful religious
practices.
By seeing and meeting them, man becomes happy.
By association with saints, evils are removed.
By association with saints, he'll is avoided.
By association with saints, man enjoys peace and comfort, both in
this world and the next.
By association with saints, man can unite with God again
He, who associates with saints, obtains the desired fruit.
By association with saints, man does not go empty handed.
The Supreme Being lives in the heart of the saints.
Nanak(Guru says), man is saved by hearing the sermons of the
saints. -6-

By association with saints, one may hear the Name of God.
By association with saints, one may sing the praises of God.
By association with saints, God cannot be forgotten.
By association with saints, man shall surely be saved.
By association with saints, man cherishes love for God.
By association with saints, God is seen in every heart.
By association with saints, we become capable of obeying the Will of God.
By association with saints, we have been saved.
By association with saints, all maladies are healed.
Nanak(Guru says), the association of Saints is obtained by very good luck. -7-

Even the Vedas(scriptures) do not know the greatness of saints.
They can only describe it as far as they have heard about it.
The greatness of saints is above the three qualities(none can compare to them).
The greatness of saints pervades every place.
There is no end to the glory of the saint.
The glory of the saint is limitless.
The glory of the saint is the highest of the high.
The glory of the saint is the greatest of the great.
The glory of the saints is possessed by themselves.
Nanak(Guru says), there is no difference between the saint and God.
-8- (7)

Salok 8
In whose heart the Immortal God resides,
And who remembers God and repeats His Name;
And who does not worship anyone but the one God;
These are the attributes if a Brahm-giani(God realized person)

Astpadi (Verse) 8

The Brahm-giani (God realized person) is unaffected by mammon,
Like the lotus flower which is not tainted by the mud under the water.
The Brahm-giani (God realized person) is free from sins and remains pious.
(He burns other's sins), just like the sun that burns and dries up things.
The Brahm-giani (God realized person) treats all men as equal;
Just as the wind blows on all, without distinction.
The Brahm-giani (God realized person) remains patient(no matter whether he is praised or abused),
Like the earth, whether one digs it up, or another smears it with sandal.
This is the attribute of The Brahm-giani (God realized person).
(His nature) is like fire, which burns the impurities of all things,
Nanak (Guru says). -1-

The Brahm-giani(God realized person) is the purest of the pure;
Like water, to which filth cannot cling.
The mind of the Brahm-giani(God realized person) is enlightened with divine light;
Like the sky over the earth.
To the Brahm-giani(God realized person) friends and foes are alike;
As he has no pride.
The Brahm-giani(God realized person) is the most exalted of the exalted;
Yet he treats himself to be the most humble person.
Only those are Brahm-giani(God realized person;
Whom God makes so, Nanak(Guru says). -2-

The Brahm-giani(God realized person) is the most humble person,
The Brahm-giani(God realized person) enjoys spiritual bliss and peace.
The Brahm-giani(God realized person) is kind to all.
The Brahm-giani(God realized person) commits no evil.
The Brahm-giani(God realized person) looks on all equally.
Nectar rains from the glance of The Brahm-giani(God realized person). -3-

The Brahm-giani(God realized person) puts his faith only on One God.

The Brahm-giani(God realized person) shall never perish.

The Brahm-giani(God realized person) is steeped in humility,

The Brahm-giani(God realized person) takes joy in doing good for others.

The Brahm-giani(God realized person) is not entangled in worldly affairs.

The Brahm-giani(God realized person) controls his wandering mind.

To the Brahm-giani(God realized person), whatever is done(by God) is the best.

The Brahm-giani(God realized person) obtains the fruit of his human life.

In the company of The Brahm-giani(God realized person) all are saved.

With the help of the Brahm-giani(God realized person), the whole world worships and remembers God, Nanak(Guru says). -4-

The Brahm-giani(God realized person) keeps in his heart, the Love for One Supreme Being.

God lives with the Brahm-giani(God realized person).

The Name of God is the support of the Brahm-giani(God realized person).

The Name of God is the family for the Brahm-giani(God realized person).

The Brahm-giani(God realized person) is always watchful(against sins).

The Brahm-giani(God realized person) renounces egoism.

The Lord of Supreme Joy resides in the heart of The Brahm-giani(God realized person).

The heart of the Brahm-giani(God realized person) is full of joy.

The Brahm-giani(God realized person) lives in peace and comfort.

The Brahm-giani(God realized person) shall never perish, Nanak(Guru) says. -5-

The Brahm-giani(God realized person) is the offspring of God.

The Brahm-giani(God realized person) loves God alone.

The Brahm-giani(God realized person) is free from worries,

The teachings of the Brahm-giani(God realized person) are pure.

He becomes Brahm-giani(God realized person), whom God makes so.

The glory of the Brahm-giani(God realized person) is great.

The sighting of a Brahm-giani(God realized person) is obtained by good luck.

Be a sacrifice to the Brahm-giani(God realized person)

Shiva(and other Gods) search for The Brahm-giani(God realized person).

Nanak(Guru says), the Brahm-giani(God realized person) himself is as(great as) God. -6-

The Brahm-giani(God realized person) is priceless.

All virtues reside within the Brahm-giani(God realized person).

Who can know the secrets of the Brahm-giani(God realized person)?

Ever bow before the Brahm-giani(God realized person).

Words cannot express the praises for a Brahm-giani(God realized person).

The Brahm-giani(God realized person) is The Lord of all.

Who can estimate the greatness of the Brahm-giani(God realized person)?

Only a Brahm-giani(God realized person) knows the divine spiritual state of the Brahm-giani(God realized person).

The Brahm-giani's(God realized person) is limitless.

Nanak(Guru says), ever bow to the Brahm-giani(God realized person). -7-

The Brahm-giani(God realized person) is the creator of the whole world.

The Brahm-giani(God realized person) lives forever and never dies.

The Brahm-giani(God realized person) is the bestowed if the path to liberation.

The Brahm-giani(God realized person) is the perfect being and sets things right.

The Brahm-giani(God realized person) is the helper if the helpless.

The Brahm-giani(God realized person) protects all.

The Brahm-giani(God realized person) owns the whole world.

The Brahm-giani(God realized person) is himself the Formless One.

The glory of The Brahm-giani(God realized person) is particular to himself.

The Brahm-giani(God realized person) is The Lord of all,

Nanak(Guru says). -8- (8)

Salok 9

He who always keeps the Name of God in his mind;
He who sees God pervading all things;
And who every moment bows to The Lord;
Is the True Saint and he causes all beings to swim(across the
worldly ocean) to liberation, Nanak(Guru says).

Astpadi(Verse) 9

He, who tongue is free from falsehood;
Whose heart yearns to see the light of God;
Who's eyes does not see the beauty of other's women;
Who serves holy men and loves saints;
Whose ears do not hear the slander of others;
Who believes himself to be the worst of all(humble);
Who, with the grace of Guru, abandons the poison of mammon;
From whose mind evil desires vanish;
And who having controlled his mind and frees himself from the five vices,
Such a saint is one in millions, Nanak(Guru says). -1-

He, upon whom God showers his grace, is the true devotee;
And he is immune from the influences of mammon.
He, who performs virtuous deeds without any desire for reward,
The religion of such a devotee is truth.
He, who has no desire of obtaining the fruits(rewards) of his deeds;
He, who always remains attached to the worship of God and sings His glories;
He, who remembers God with utmost love with mind and body;
He, who is merciful to all;
He, who enshrines the Name of God in his heart, and makes others utter and remember it;
Is the true saint, and attains the highest spiritual status, Nanak,(Guru says). -2-

He is Bhaghauti(The worshiper of God), who sincerely loves God
Who abandons the society of sinners;
Who removes duality from his mind;
Who worships God, realizing Him to be present everywhere;
Who sheds the filth of sins and joins the company of saints;
The wisdom of such a Bhaghauti(The worshiper of God), is pure.
He, who always serves(worships) God;
He. Who dedicates his soul and body to the devotion of God;
He, who keeps God's divine instructions in his heart;
Such a Bhaghauti(The worshiper of God), realizes God, Nanak(Guru says). -3-

He, who awakens his mind, is the true Pandit(priest);
And he, who searches for the Name of God within his heart.
He, who drinks the sweet juice of the Name of God;
The world get spiritual uplifting from such a Pandit(priest).
He, who keeps the divine instructions of God in his heart,
Is such a Pandit(priest), who will not take birth again.
He, who understands the true origin of the scriptures,
He, who realizes that the visible world exists(by support of the Invisible Being);
Who gives divine instructions to all the four castes;
Nanak(Guru says), forever bow to such a Pandit(priest). -4-

The Name of God is the Fundamental spell and imparts divine knowledge to all;
Anyone from the four castes may repeat the Name of God;
Whoever repeats God's Name will attain salvation;
But only some rare men attain it, in the society if saints.
If by His(God's) grace, he makes the Name reside in their hearts;
Even the brutes, fools, sprites and stone-hearted will be saved.
The Name of God is the medicine for all ills;
And singing the praises of God, brings true and divine joy.
The Name cannot be obtained in any other way, or through any religious ceremonies or rituals;
Nanak(Guru says), he, for whom such a Destiny is already recorded, obtains the Name of God. -5-

He, in whose heart God resides;
Can truly be called the servant of God.
He realizes the all-pervading supreme soul of God.
He realizes God, because he treats himself as a slave of the slaves of God.
He, who believes that God is ever-present and close to him;
Such a servant is acceptable at God's court
He, Himself confers His Grace on his own servant.
Such a servant obtains all divine knowledge.
He, who resides with all and yet remains detached from all;
This is the way of a true servant of God, Nanak(Guru says). -6-

He, who obeys in his heart with pleasure, the Will of God;
Is called a liberated one, even while alive.
Joy and grief are alike to him;
He is ever happy because he never gets separated(from God).
Gold and mud are alike for him;
Nectar and poison are alike for him;
Honor and disgrace are alike for him;
King and pauper are alike for him;
Whatever God does, is the best(for him);
Nanak(Guru says), such a person is called a liberated one. -7-

The entire creation belongs to the Supreme being.
The creatures are called by different names according to the places that they are placed.
God Himself has power to do and cause others to do;
Whatever pleases God, must happen.
God pervades all,
The plays of the Supreme being cannot be described
Light dawns on a person according to the understanding imparted by God.
The Supreme Being is Himself the doer, and is immortal.
God is ever, ever and ever merciful.
By remembering and remembering Him. Nanak(Guru says) one gets supreme joy. -8- (9)

Salok 10

**Countless men praise God, but his limits are endless.
Nanak(Guru says), God has created His creation and with
creatures of many kinds and species.**

Astpadi(Verse) 10

Many millions are worshippers of God;
Many millions are performers of religious and worldly duties;
Many millions reside at places of pilgrimage ;
Many millions wander in forests;
Many millions listen to the scriptures;
Many millions perform difficult penances;
Many millions meditate in their hearts;
Many millions interpret religious poems;
Many millions remember and meditate on new Names of God;
Nanak(Guru says), none can find the limits of the Creator -1-

Many millions are proud;
Many millions are blinded with ignorance;
Many millions are misers and stone-hearted;
Many millions are unconcerned and heartless;
Many millions steal other's property;
Many millions slander others;
Many millions work hard to gain wealth;
Many millions wander in foreign lands.
Wherever God appoints the created ones to work, they do that.
Nanak(Guru says), God alone knows the plan of his creation. -2-

Many millions are seers, holy men and ascetics.
Many millions are kings enjoying worldly pleasures.
Many millions of birds and serpents have been created.
Many millions of trees and stones have been created.
Many millions are the winds, water, and fires.
Many millions are the countries and regions of the earth.
Many millions are the moons, suns and stars.
Many millions are demi-gods, demons and heavenly beings with
kingly umbrellas,
God has strung the entire creation under His Command.

Nanak(Guru says), He saves those whom he pleases(in accordance with his laws). -3-

Many millions possess the qualities of ambition, darkness and greed.
Many millions are the religious scriptures.
Many millions of jewels have been created in the oceans.
Many millions are animals of different kinds.
Many millions of creatures with long lives have been created.
Many millions of hills and golden mountains have been created.
Many millions of spirits of different types have been created
}Many millions are sprites, ghosts, pigs and tigers.
God is near to all, yet he seems far away.
Nanak(Guru says), God pervades all, yet he is separate from all. -4-

Many millions live in nether regions.
Many millions live in heaven and hell.
Many millions take birth, live, and die
Many millions wander in transmigration.
Many millions are fed while seated comfortably.
Many millions have to toil and work hard.
Many millions are made wealthy,
Many millions remain perturbed and are eager to get rich.
Wherever God wills, He places them.
Nanak(Guru says), every thing is in God's hands. -5-

Many millions are detached from the world;
Who are absorbed in the meditation of God's Name.
Many millions are searching for God:
And realize God in their hearts.
Many millions are thirsty for God's sight;
And God, the Imperishable One, meets them.
Many millions pray for the company of true devotees;
And therein they get true love for the Supreme being.
They, with whom God is pleased;
Are forever blessed, Nanak(Guru says). -6-

Many millions are the regions and fields of creation.
Many millions are the skies and the worlds.

Many millions are taking birth.
The world was spread out in different shapes.
Many times the world stage has folded and unfolded;
God alone existed, through all time.
Many millions of creatures of various kinds have been created;
They originated from God, and in God they are absorbed.
No one knows His limits.
Nanak(Guru says), God is in all. -7-

Many millions are the devotees of the Supreme Being;
Whose minds are enlightened.
Many millions are the knower of the True Being(God),
And forever look to the One.
Many millions drink the nectar of the Name;
And become immortal.
Many millions sing the excellences of the Name;
They remain absorbed in the divine bliss and are at peace.
God always remembers and protects His devotees
Nanak(Guru says), such ones are dear to God. -8- (10)

Salok 11
God alone is the doer(cause) of all acts and there is none else.
Nanak(Guru says), I am a sacrifice to Him,
Who pervades waters, lands, nether regions and skies.

Astpadi(Verse) 11

God alone is capable of doing everything;
Whatever pleases Him, comes to pass.
In the twinkling of an eye, He can create and destroy the World.
There is no limit to His powers.
He creates the creation by His Will and supports it;
By His Order, the world is created and absorbed into Himself.
By His Order, the high and low perform their occupations.
By His Order, different kinds of acts and dramas are played out.
Having created the creation, He beholds His greatness.
Nanak(Guru says), God is contained in all. -1-

If God is pleased, man obtains salvation.
If God is pleased, He can make a stonehearted person swim across the worldly ocean.
If God is pleased, He restores life to the lifeless.
If God is pleased, man utters His praises.
If God is pleased, He saves the sinners.
He does whatever pleases Him, in accordance with His Will.
He is The Lord of this world and the next one.
The Omniscient Lord performs His plays and enjoys His creation
He gets done, whatever He wants.
Nanak(Guru) says, there is no other like Him. -2-

What can man do by himself?
Whatever pleases God that gets done.
If it were in man's power, he would get things done his way;
He would do whatever He likes.
Because of ignorance, man is attached to the poison of sins.
If he is wise, he would save himself.
Misled by duality, the mind wanders in ten directions.
I'm the blink of an eye, the mind returns back after wandering in four corners.
He(the devotee), upon whom he confers His grace ;
Such a devotee shall get absorbed in the Name of God, Nanak(Guru says). -3-

In a moment, God can confer a kingdom on a lowly being;
The Supreme being is the Protector and Cherisher of the poor.
A man, who is fully obscure;
Can be made famous in no time by God.
Upon whom God confers His grace,
Such a being is not accountable and judged by God.
Body and Soul are His property.
God's light shines in every heart.
He Himself has built the structure of the world.
Nanak(Guru), lives by beholding His Greatness -4-

Man has no power in his hands,
The Lord is the doer and cause of all.
The helpless man works on accordance with His Will;
Only that which pleases God, shall happen.
Man is sometimes elevated and sometimes debased.
Sometimes he is depressed and sometimes happy.
Sometimes he engages in slandering of blaming others.
Sometimes he is elated.
Sometimes he obtains the divine knowledge;
Nanak(Guru says), God Himself unites with Him those that are
pleasing to Him. -5-

Sometimes man dances in different directions,
Sometimes he sleeps night and day.
Sometimes he exhibits great anger.
Sometimes he becomes the most humble person.
Sometimes he sits on a throne(in comfort),
Sometimes he wears the attire of a pauper.
Sometimes he acquires evil reputation,
Sometimes he is regarded as very good.
As God keeps him, so does man live his life.
By the grace of the Guru, such a one utters the Truth, Nanak(Guru
says). -6-

Sometimes he gives religious sermons like a priest.
Sometimes he becomes silent and practices contemplation.
Sometimes he takes bath at places of pilgrimage.
Sometimes as a seeker he preaches divine knowledge.
The Soul sometimes wanders as a worm, elephant or moth.
And wanders in many wombs in the mazes of life.
As a player, he plays many roles(according to God's Will);
As God pleases, so He makes the man dance.
What pleases God, must happen.
Nanak(Guru says), there is none other than Him -7-

Sometimes man obtains the society of saints;
From where he does not return again.
The divine light comes and shines in his heart;
And this awakened state never perishes.

The devotee's body and soul are dyed with the love of One God;
He shall ever abide with the Supreme Being,
As water blends with water,
So does the soul of the devotee merge with the Supreme Soul.
Transmigration ceases and final rest is obtained
Nanak(Guru says), I am ever and ever a sacrifice to God. -8- (11)

Salok 12
He, who is humble, lives a happy life.
But the proud ones who have high status, are consumed by their
pride, Nanak(Guru says).

Astpadi(Verse) 12
He, in whose heart the pride of riches exists,
Is like an animal headed for hell
Who prides in the beauty of youth,
Shall be worm as a filthy worm.
He who considers himself to be virtuous,
Shall take birth and die over and over again.
He, who is proud of his riches and lands,
Is an idiot who is both blind and ignorant.
He, in whose heart God causes humility to reside,
Shall attain salvation in this life, and shall get divine peace in God's
court, Nanak(Guru says).-1-

He, who becomes wealthy and takes pride in his riches should
realize,
That not even a straw will accompany him in the end.
The person, who relies on his huge army and men,
Shall be destroyed in a moment.
He, who thinks himself to be the strongest of all,
Shall, in the blink of an eye, become ashes.
The proud man does not care for anybody,
The Divine Judge shall thoroughly disgrace him in the end.
He, whose pride is effaced by the true Guru;
Shall be accepted in God's court, Nanak(Guru says). -2-

He, who performs millions of religious deeds, and takes pride in it,
Incurs only the trouble and receives no fruit
He, who is proud of his different acts of penances,
Shall taste heaven and hell over and over again, never attaining
union with God.
If the heart is not softened despite making many efforts,
Then how can such a person go to God's court?
He, who calls himself to be virtuous;
Goodness shall not even come near him.
He, who becomes the dust of the feet of all(humble);
Shall attain true glory and fame, Nanak(Guru says).-3-

As long as man thinks that something can be done by him;
So long he cannot find any peace.
As long as he thinks that all things are done through his effort
So long he shall wander in transmigration.
As long as he classifies some people to be his friend, and some his
enemy,
So long shall his mind not be stable
As long as man remains attached to worldly love.
So long shall the divine judge punish him.
The chains of mammon are broken by God's grace.
The pride of man is removed by the kindness of the Guru,
Nanak(Guru says). -4-

Man earns thousands and runs for much more;
He is never satisfied and he goes on gathering riches.
He goes on enjoying evil pleasures,
And is never satisfied, and keeps seeking more till he finally dies.
No man can ever be satiated without having contentment;
And all his acts are fruitless, like the illusion of a dream.
By attaching with the Name of God, all comforts and true happiness
is obtained;
But these are obtained by a few, by good destiny.
God is all-powerful to do anything He Wills,
Nanak(Guru says), ever and forever repeat His Name. -5-

The Creator Himself does and gets things done.

There is no power in man's hand.
Man becomes what God wants;
God is everything.
Whatever has been created, is by His Will;
God is far from all, yet he is near.
He understands, sees, and judges everything.
He Himself is One, yet His manifestations are countless.
He neither dies, nor is born.
Nanak(Guru says), he is diffused in the entire creation.-6-

He Himself gives instructions and He understands them.
He Himself blends with His creation.
He Himself had created His own expanse.
Everything is His, and He is the Creator.
Can anyone be created without Him?
The One God is present at every place.
He himself is the player of the world drama.
God is present in all minds and all minds reside in Him.
Nanak(Guru says), His worth cannot be described. -7-

God is True, the Ultimate Truth.
By the kindness of the True Guru, some can know this truth.
Whatever He has created, is also True.
Some rare and fortunate people come to know this.
O Lord, Excellent, Excellent, Excellent is Your Form.
Exquisitely beautiful, boundless and incomparable.
Pure, Pure, Pure, is Your Word.
When uttered of when heard, it settles every mind.
Your Name is the Holiest of the Holy;
In the mind of Nanak(Guru), there is love and devotion for the Holy
Name and Nanak(Guru) remembers to cherish it. -8- (12)

Salok 13
He, who gets the protection of the true saints, will be saved.
The slanderer of the saints will be born over and over again,
Nanak(Guru says).

38

By slandering the saint, the slanderer's life is shortened.
By slandering the saint, the slanderer does not escape death
By slandering the saint, all happiness vanishes.
By slandering the saint, the slanderer falls into hell.
By slandering the saint, the slanderer's wisdom becomes clouded.
By slandering the saint, the slanderer is deprived of fame.
He, who is cursed by the saint, cannot be saved by anybody.
By slandering the saint, all places touched by the slanderer becomes polluted.
If the merciful saint shows mercy,
Only then the slanderer will be saved by joining the society of the saints, Nanak(Guru says).-1-

By slandering the saint, the slanderer strays from the path.
By slandering the saint, the slanderer shouts like a crow.
By slandering the saint, the slanderer takes birth as a snake.
By slandering the saint, the slanderer takes birth as a worm.
By slandering the saint, the slanderer burns in the fire of greed.
By slandering the saint, the slanderer becomes a cheat.
By slandering the saint, the slanderer's influence vanishes.
By slandering the saint, the slanderer becomes the meanest of the mean.
The slanderer of the saint does not get protection anywhere.
Yet, if it pleases the saint, the slanderer may obtain salvation, Nanak(Guru says).-2-

The slanderer of the saint , is a great evildoer.
The slanderer of the saint dies not get rest even for a moment.
The slanderer of the saint is a heartless criminal.
The slanderer of the saint, is the accursed of God.
The slanderer of the saint loses his kingdom,
The slanderer of the saint becomes miserable and poor
The slanderer of the saint gets all diseases.
The slanderer of the saint suffers separation from God.
The slanderer of the saint is one of the biggest sins.
Nanak(Guru says), if it pleases the saint, even the slanderer may obtain salvation. -3-

The slanderer of the saint is impure.
The slanderer of the saint is the friend if none.
The slanderer of the saint shall be punished.
All will abandon the slanderer if the saints.
The slanderer of the saint is full of pride.
The slanderer of the saint always commits evil deeds.
The slanderer of the saint continues experiencing birth and death.
The slanderer of the saint is deprived of peace and pleasure.
The slanderer of the saint dies not get shelter anywhere.
Nanak(Guru says), if the saint so likes, he may join with him.-4-

The slanderer of the saint breaks down in the middle.
The slanderer of the saint does not succeed in anything.
The slanderer of the saint wanders in delusion.
The slanderer of the saint is led on the wrong path.
The slanderer of the saint is hollow from within.
Just like a lifeless corpse without breath.
The pedigree of the slanderer of the saint withers away.
He eats the fruits of what he has sown.
No one will protect the slanderer of the saints;
Nanak(Guru says), if the saint wants so, he may save him.-5-

The slanderer of the saint cries loudly;
Just as the fish twists in absence of water.
The slanderer of the saint shall never be satiated;
Just as the fire is not satiated with firewood.
The slanderer of the saint is left alone;
Just like the barren stalk is abandoned in the field.
The slanderer of the saint is void of truth.
The slanderer of the saint always speaks lies.
This is the fruit of the sins of the slanderer from the beginning.
Nanak(Guru says), whatever pleases God, must happen. -6-

The slanderer of the saint becomes deformed.
The slanderer of the saint shall be punished in God's court.
The slanderer of the saint forever gasps;
The slanderer of the saint is neither dead nor alive.
No desire if the slanderer of the saint shall be fulfilled.

The slanderer of the saint leaves (the world) disappointed.
By slandering the saint, no one will be satiated.
Man's habit is formed according to his intentions
No one can erase his destiny.
Nanak(Guru says), the True One alone knows this secret. -7-

All living beings belong to Him, and He can do anything.
Forever now to Him.
Go on praising God day and night.
Remember Him with every breath.
Everything happens in accordance with His Will.
Everyone becomes such, as us willed by God.
God Himself plays His own play.
Who else can advise Him?
He bestows the gift of His Name to those, upon whom he is merciful.
Nanak(Guru says), such ones are very fortunate. -8- (13)

Salok 14
Abandon cleverness and remember God, the True King.
Keep in your hearts the yearning in One God, and your troubles, duality and fear will vanish, Nanak(Guru says).

Astpadi(Verse) 14
Realize that all reliance on man is useless.
God alone is the Giver of all.
By whose gifts we remain satiated;
And no more desire arises.
God Himself causes death or saves life;
Nothing is in Man's hand.
Happiness comes by accepting God's Will.
String His Name and forever remember Him.
Remember, remember, remember such a God;
And then, no obstacles shall come in your path, Nanak(Guru says)-1-

Praise the Formless One in your heart.
O my mind, perform virtuous deeds.
Drink the nectar of the Name with your tongue;
And in doing so, make your soul happy forever.
Behold with your eyes God's drama,
In the society of saints, the need for love for any other disappears.
Walk with your feet towards the direction of God.
By remembering God and repeating His Name, all sins are erased.
Perform good deeds with your hands and hear his praises with your ears;
Nanak(Guru says), in this way you shall shine in the court of God.-2-

Fortunate are those in this world,
Who ever and ever, sings the praises of God.
They, who meditate on God's Name,
Are truly rich in this world.
They, who sincerely utter God's Name with heart and mind,
Know them to be forever happy.
He, who recognizes only One God,
Comes to know all about this world and next.
He, whose mind is attached to thc Name,
Realizes God, Nanak(Guru says). -3-

He, who comes to know his own self(self realization) through the Guru's grace,
Know it that his thirst and desires are quenched.
The devotee, who praises God when in the company of holy men;
Shall be immune from all diseases.
He, who sings the divine hymns day and night;
Becomes free from all desires even while living with his family.
He, who puts all his hopes on God alone;
His noose of death will be cut.
He, who has great yearning to see God,
Will have no suffering, Nanak(Guru says). -4-

He, who remembers God in his Heart;
Is a true saint and never wavers.
He, to whom God shows mercy,
From whom should he be afraid?
To him, God appears as He in fact is;
And he shall see God contained in all creation.
By thinking, thinking and thinking(about God), the devotee succeeds;
And comes to realize the ultimate reality by the Guru's grace.
When I look, I see that God is the cause if all things.
He is the all pervading Supreme Soul and also the visible world,
Nanak(Guru says). -5-

Neither anyone takes birth, nor anyone dies;
God Himself plays His drama(of creating and destroying).
That which comes and goes, which is visible and invisible;
The whole creation is supported by and works under his command.
He Himself is contained in all.
He makes and unmakes in various ways by using many devices.
God is Intangible and Immortal;
He creates the entire World.
He is Unseen, Inscrutable and Glorious.
Nanak(Guru says), man can only repeat His Name, if He Himself causes to do so. -6-

They, who have realized God, become famous and honorable;
The whole world will be saved by their sermons.
God's servants are capable of saving all,
God's servants are capable of removing other's sorrow and pain.
The Merciful One unites his devotees with Him.
They, who repeat the Name of God under the Guru's instructions, become happy.
That man is caused to serve such true saints,
Upon whom, through good luck, God showers His grace.
They, who repeat the Name, acquire a blissful state through a detached mind.
Nanak(Guru says), consider such devotees to be the most pious -7-

Whatever the devotee does, he does for the love of God.

He ever and ever resides with God.
Whatever happens, he accepts it as the Will of God.
He believes Him(God) to be the Doer of everything.
Whatever God dies, is pleasing to the devotee.
As God is, so He appears to them.
They remain absorbed in Him, from whom they have sprung
They become the treasure of happiness and are worthy of this status.
He Himself honors Himself (by honoring his devotees);
Nanak(Guru says), realize that God and His servants are one. -8-
(14)

Salok 15

God possesses all powers, and He knows the pains and troubles of all.
By remembering Him, salvation is obtained; I am a sacrifice to Him, Nanak(Guru says).

Astpadi(Verse) 15

God joins the broken string(unites the deserted ones with Him).
He cherishes all living beings.
In His heart, there is concern for all.
Nobody comes dejected from Him.
O my mind, ever repeat God's Name.
He is imperishable and is in all.
Nothing can be done by the mortal's own efforts;
Even though he may desire it a hundred times.
Without God, nothing will be if any use to you.
Nanak(Guru says), salvation is attained by repeating the Name of the One God. -1-

If someone is handsome, he should not be proud of it;
Because it is the light of God that shines in every body.
Why should man become proud, if he is wealthy?
Since all the wealth is provided by God.
If anyone is called a great hero;
What can he do without obtaining power from God?

If by giving, someone is called a benefactor,
One must recognize that it is God who is the Giver of all.
He, whose disease if pride is eradicated by the Guru's grace,
Is always healthy and free from all diseases, Nanak(Guru says). -2-

As a pillar supports the roof of a house;
So does the Word of the Guru support the mind.
Just as a stone placed on a boat can swim across the river,
So does man swim across the world ocean, by clinging to the Guru's feet(heeding his guidance).
Like the lamp that throws light in the darkness,
So does man radiate with joy on seeing the Guru.
As a lost man in the wilderness finds the way,
So does the divine light shine within him, when he joins the society of the Guru.
I want the dust from the feet of such a Revered Guru;
O God, please fulfill this desire, Nanak(Guru says). -3-

O foolish mind, why do you weep(when in trouble)?
You have to reap the harvest of your deeds, according to destiny.
God is the dispenser of pleasure and pain(based on your deeds).
Abandon other supports, and remember only Him.
Take it with joy, whatever He does.
O ignorant man, why do you wander aimlessly?
What things came with you(at birth)?
That you are so attached to worldly pleasures, like a moth?
Repeat God's Name in your heart.
And go back to the true home with dignity, Nanak(Guru says). -4-
The merchandise that you came to obtain in this world;
Is the Name of God, which can be found in the Guru's house.
Abandon egoism and get God's Name by surrendering your mind.
And then meditate on the Name in your heart.
Load the merchandise of the Name and set forth with the true saints;
And abandon all entanglements caused by evil.
Everyone will then congratulate and honor you.
And your face will be bright in the court of God.
Rare is the one who does such a trade;
Nanak(Guru says), I am ever a sacrifice to such a devotee. -5-

Wash the feet if the Guru and drink the water;
Sacrifice your soul to the Guru.
Bathe yourself in the dust of the feet of the Guru.
Become a sacrifice to the Guru.
The service of a Guru is obtained through good luck;
Sing the praises of God in the Guru's company.
The Guru protects the devotee from many dangers and difficulties.
Taste the sweet nectar by singing the praises of God.
He, who takes the shelter of the Saint,
Obtains all comforts, Nanak(Guru says). -6-

God can restore life to the dead;
He gives support to the needy.
All treasures are inherent in His glance.
All obtain only what has been destined for them.
He is Omnipotent and everything belongs to Him.
There neither has been not ever will be anyone except Him.
O man! Repeat His Name, over and over, day and night.
This is the most sacred and exalted deed.
He, upon whom God kindly confers His Name,
Becomes pure, Nanak(Guru says). -7-

He, in whose heart exists the faith for the Guru;
Remembers God in his heart.
He is known as a saint in the three worlds;
On whose heart resides the One God.
His way of life and deeds are true,
Truth is in his heart and he utters truth with his mouth.
His vision is true and he sees the True One present every where.
He believes that God pervades all, and all are His manifestations.
He, who understands the Supreme One, is true;
Will be merged with Him, Nanak(Guru says). -8- (15)

Salok 16
God has no form, outline or color.
He is unaffected by the three qualities of Maya(mammon).
He causes one to know Him, with whom He is pleased,
Nanak(Guru says).

Astpadi(Verse) 16
Keep the immortal God in your mind.
Abandon attachment with man.
There is no one above God.
He exists in all beings.
He Himself is Sensible and Wise.
He is Unfathomable, Profound and most Sagacious.
O Supreme Being, Supreme Lord, Caretaker of all;
Ocean of Mercy, kind Pardoner;
Grant that I may fall at the feet of your saints;
This is my utmost desire, Nanak(Guru says). -1-

God is the fulfilled of desires and capable of helping those who seek
His protection.
What He has written(inscribed as Destiny), that will happen.
In the blink of an eye, He can destroy and create.
No one, except He, knows His inner secret.
Present at His abode are happiness and joy;
It is heard that all things are present at His abode.
He is the King of Kings, and Yogi of Yogis.
Among Ascetics, He is the Supreme Ascetic, and among family-
men, He is a family-man.
The saints have obtained happiness by remembering and
remembering Him.
No one has known the limits of such a Being, Nanak(Guru says). -2-

His world play is limitless.
All demigods have grown tired searching for the same.
How can a son know about his father's birth?
God has strung all on His own string.
Devotees, upon whom God gives true wisdom and divine
knowledge;
Only those servants(devotees) can remember and worship His Name.

Those who are lead astray with the three qualities of
Maya(mammon),
Are born and die over and over again.
High and low status are His creation,
Man can only realize this, if He ordains so. -3-

God's forms and colors are of various kinds;
He assumes various guises, and yet He has one form.
God has manifested in various ways;
God is imperishable and is One.
He performs various plays in a moment;
The Perfect One fills all places.
God created the creation in various ways;
He alone knows His own worth.
All hearts and all places are His.
Nanak(Guru says), live by uttering His Name. -4-

All creation is sustained by the Name.
The world and the regions are supported by the Name.
The Holy Scriptures are supported by the Name.
The hearing of Divine Sermons is dependent on the Name.
The firmament and the nether regions are supported by The Name.
All the bodies are supported by The Name.
The three worlds and fourteen spheres are supported by The Name.
By hearing the Name with devotion, man will be saved.
He, to whom God mercifully attaches with His Name;
Shall obtain salvation by attaining the fourth status(unaffected by
mammon), Nanak(Guru says). -5-

The Form of God is true, and His place is true.
He is the True and Supreme Being.
His acts are true, and His words are true.
The True Being pervades all.
His deeds are true and His creation is true.
The root of all is True, and what springs from it, is True.
God's deeds are the purest of the pure.
He who understands this, finds joy.
The True Name of God is the giver of comforts and joy.
Man obtains this faith from the Guru(Nanak says). -6-

The words and sermons of the Saint are true.
They, in whose hearts these enter, are also true.
If anyone comes to know the value of the Love for the eternal God,
He will attain salvation by uttering the Name of God.
God is True and all His creation is True.
He Himself knows his own limits.
God is the Creator of this world.
Do not think anybody else to be the caretaker of this world.
One created by God, cannot estimate Him.
Whatever pleases God, will Happen, Nanak(Guru says). -7-

Whoever has understood the Greatness of God, becomes wonder struck.
He who has realized God, gets wondrous spiritual bliss.
The true servants remain saturated in the love of God.
They obtain everything through Guru's Words.
They are givers of comfort and can destroy all misery;
In whose company the entire world gets salvation.
He, who has the privilege to perform service of the devotee of God, is fortunate
In the association of the devotee, one develops devotion with the One Supreme Being.
The devotee of God always sings His praises.
With the grace of the Guru,
He gets rewarded, Nanak(Guru says). -8- (16)

Salok
Truth(God) prevailed in the beginning, before the ages began.
God is present Now, and Forever will be.

Astpadi(Verse) 17
God's feet(path) is True, and whoever touches(follows) them become True also.
The worship of God is True, and the worshipers of God are True.

The sight of God is True and those who obtain it are True.
The Name of God is True and those who meditate on it are True.
God is True, and all that He sustains are True.
God is by Himself all-virtuous and is the fountain of virtues.
The Word of God is True and the one who utters it is also True.
Focusing one's attention on God is True, and the hearing if His praises is also True
One, who realizes the existence of God, realizes the truth of His creation.
Nanak(Guru says), God is ever True and True. -1-

He, who believes that God, Whose firm is true, is also present in his heart,
Comes to know the Root of all, and the Doer of all.
He, in whose heart the belief and faith in God resides;
The true Divine Knowledge is revealed in his mind
He then lives, free from all fear;
And gets merged in Him, from Whom he came.
Just as one thing is mixed with another of the same kind;
It cannot be distinguished as separate from the other.
Only a man with divine understanding can understand this.
Nanak(Guru says), man blends with God upon meeting Him. -2-

God's devotee follows His order.
God's devotee forever worships Him.
God's devotee keeps faith in God.
God's devotee's conduct and way of life is pure.
God's devotee realizes that God is ever present with Him.
God's devotee is dyed with the Name of God.
God cherishes His devotee.
The Formless One saves his honor.
He, upon whom God confers His grace, becomes His devotee.
Nanak(Guru says), such a servant remembers God with every breath.
-3-

God covers His devotee(faults) with a veil(forgives and pardons).
He protects His devotee.
He confers glory on His devotee.

He enables His devotee to repeat the Name.
He Himself preserves the honor of His devotees.
No one knows His condition and limits.
No one comes close to God's devotee.
God's devotee is the highest of the high.
He, who God applied to His service,
Becomes known in the ten directions(everywhere), Nanak(Guru says). -4-

The small ant in which He(God) has infused His power;
Can reduced to ashes armies of millions.
As long as He does not remove the breath of the being;
He protects and preserves the being with outstretched hands.
Man makes all sorts of efforts;
But his plans remain fruitless without God's grace.
No one else can cause death or preserve life;
He is the Preserver of all beings.
O mortal, why are you anxious(thinking of your schemes)?
Remember forever, the wonderful God, Nanak(Guru says), -5-

Repeat God's Name over and over again.
Drink the Nectar of the Name and satiate the soul and body.
The true devotee, who is blessed with the jewel of the Name;
Does not look up to anyone, but God.
The Name is his wealth, beauty and joy;
The Name is his comfort and companion.
He, who is satiated with the nectar of the Name,
His soul and body get merged with the Name.
Meditate on the Name, whether standing, sitting or sleeping;
Is the true occupation of God's devotee, Nanak(Guru says). -6-

Utter the praises of God with your tongue, day and night.
God has bestowed this gift on His devotees.
They meditate and worship God with true love,
And remain absorbed in the Lord.
The true devotee regards all happening as the Will of God.
He accepts the commands of his God.
How can I describe His virtues?

I can't even describe one if His excellences.
They, who live with the presence of God in their minds, all the time;
Such devotees are perfect, Nanak(Guru says). -7-

O mind, obtain the shelter of such beings,
Surrender your soul and mind to them.
The devotee, who recognizes God,
Becomes the giver of all things.
You will find all comforts in his shelter.
By beholding him, all your sins will be wiped away.
Leave all other cleverness;
And attach yourself to the service of such a person.
There will then be no coming and going(transmigration of soul).
Ever worship his feet, Nanak(Guru says). -8- (17)

Salok 18

One, who knows the True Supreme Being, is called the True Guru.
The devotee is saved, associating with Him and singing God's praises.

Astpadi(Verse) 18
The True Guru looks after his disciple.
The Guru is always kind to his disciple.
The Guru removes the filth of evil thoughts from his disciple.
Through his instructions, he repeats God's Name.
The True Guru cuts the disciples bonds with mammon;
The Guru's disciples steers away from evil deeds.
The True Guru bestows the wealth of the Name on the disciple.
The disciple of the Guru is very fortunate.
The True Guru adjusts this life and the next for the disciple.
Nanak(Guru says), the True Guru loves his disciple like his own life.
-1-
The disciple, who remains in the path of the Guru,
Who faithfully obeys the orders if the Guru;
Who treats himself as if he's worth nothing,
Who forever remembers the Name of God in his heart;

Who surrenders his mind to the True Guru;
Such devotees get all their affairs accomplished.
He, who serves the True Guru without any desire for reward;
Shall attain God.
He, upon whom God becomes kind,
Obtains the instructions of the True Guru, Nanak(Guru says). -2-

The disciple, whose devotion and sincerity wins the confidence of the Guru,
Comes to know the Supremacy of the Supreme Being.
He is the True Guru, in whose heart the Name of God resides.
I am a sacrifice to such a Guru, many times.
He is the Giver of life to all beings;
He has a blissful state of love for the Supreme Being, day and night.
The holy man is absorbed in God, and God is in the holy man.
There is no doubt that the True Guru and God are One.
The True Guru is not obtained by a thousand plans.
Such a Guru is obtained by very good luck, Nanak(Guru says). -3-

The sight of the Guru purifies the one who sees;
By touching his feet, true and pious conduct is achieved.
In his association, the praises of God are sung;
And he gets access to the Supreme Lord.
On hearing the Guru's Word, the devotee's ears gets satisfaction.
The mind is content and the soul is at peace.
The True Guru is perfect and his teachings are eternal truth.
He, on whom the True Guru looks with an ambrosial glance, becomes a saint.
The True Guru's glories are countless and priceless.
Nanak(Guru says), whoever the True Guru desires, is blessed with the union(of God). -4-

The tongue is one, but it's praises for The Lord are manifold.
He is the True Being, with perfect judgment.
A mortal can never succeed in describing Him with words.
He is Inaccessible, Incomprehensible and Immune from all desires.
He does not live by food, He is enemy of none, and He is the Giver of happiness.

No one can assess his value.
Many saints always make obeisance to The Lord;
And worship Him in their hearts.
I am ever a sacrifice to my True Guru.
By whose grace, the Name of God is repeated, Nanak(Guru says). -
5-

Rare are those who obtain the Divine taste of God's Name.
And he, who drinks this Nectar, becomes immortal(no more transmigration).
Such a person will never perish;
Within whose heart, the excellent Lord enters.
He utters God's Name during the eight watches(round the clock).
He gives True instructions to his devotees.
He is unaffected by worldly love or desires.
He keeps the One God forever in his heart.
In whose minds the divine lamp(of the Name) comes to shine in the darkness;
Doubts, falsehood and pain caviars from their minds, Nanak(Guru says). -6-

In the midst if heat, coolness has been restored;
True joy comes and pains glee away.
The terror of endless births and deaths is removed.
All this is attained through the instructions of the True Guru.
All fear ceases and the devotee leads a life free from fear;
And all the troubles and pain also vanish from the mind.
The Guru has shown mercy on his devotee.
The devotee repeats the Name of God in the company of the Guru.
Peace of mind is attained and transmigration has ceased;
By listening to the praises of God, Nanak(Guru says). -7-

God does not possess the qualities, yet He possesses all the qualities.
His power has fashioned the whole world.
God Himself performs His plays.
He Himself knows His value.
There is no other than God;
It is One God that pervades and is present in all.
He is present everywhere in all forms and colors.
This knowledge of God is attained by association with the saints.

He infused His Light and Power into the creation after creating it.
Nanak(Guru says), I am forever a sacrifice to Him. -8- (18)

Salok 19
Nothing will accompany you in the end except the worship of God;
All worldly things are left behind.
Nanak(Guru says), the true earning of wealth is the repetition of God's Name(worship and remembrance).

Astpadi(Verse) 19

Meditate on God in the company of saints;
Remember the One(God) and take shelter of His Name.
O friend, forget all other acts(they are useless).
Keep the lotus feet(Divine Word) of God in your heart.
He alone is the Doer and the One that gets everything Done.
Acquire God's Name with determination;
Gather this wealth and become a fortunate one.
This is the pure sermon of the saints.
Keep hope of One God in your heart.
All your maladies will be healed, Nanak(Guru says). -1-

Wealth, for which you run after in all directions;
That wealth, you can obtain, by serving God.
The comforts that you always desire;
Those comforts you can obtain by cherishing God, in the company of saints.
The glory you seek by performing good deeds;
That glory you can obtain by hastening to get God's protection.
The maladies(evils) which are incurable by many remedies;
They will be cured by taking the medicine of God's Name.
God's Name is the treasure of all treasures.
Utter it, and you will attain acceptance in God's court, Nanak(Guru says). -2-

Awaken your mind with God's Name;
The mind that wanders in ten directions will finally obtain true peace.
No obstacles will come to Him,
In whose Heart God resides.
The age of Kal(Dark Age) is hot, the Name of God is cool.
Remember and remember(The Name) and obtain comfort.
Fear vanishes and hopes are fulfilled.
By sincere loving worship, the mind is enlightened.
In the devotee's mind, the Immortal comes to reside.
And the noose of death is cut, Nanak(God says). -3-

The one who utters the Name, becomes True.
Those who dwell in falsehood, get engaged in births and deaths.
Transmigration can only end by serving God.
Abandon your ego and seek the protection of the Guru.
In this way, the true goal of human life is achieved.
Remember God, the true support of the Soul.
By various other methods, the mortal cannot be saved from transmigration.
Not even by studying all the scriptures.
Sincerely worship God with devotion.
And you will get what your heart desires, Nanak(Guru says). -4-

Wealth will not accompany you;
O mind, why are you attached to it?
Children, friends, family and spouse;
Tell, who will accompany you after death?
Dominance, worldly joy and immense wealth;
Those who are entangled in these, how can they get salvation?
Horses, elephants, chariots, equipages;
Are false shows and false displays.
Man does not know and recognize the true Giver.
Forgetting God's Name, he will repent, Nanak(Guru says). -5-

Seek the advice if the Guru,
Without true devotion, even wise men have been drowned(in delusion).

O my dear mind, worship and dedicate yourself to God.
This way, both mind and soul will become pure.
Keep God's word in your mind;
The sins of many births will vanish.
Repeat His Holy Name and encourage others to do so.
Attain salvation by hearing It(Name), uttering It and abiding by It.
God's Name is the real property.
Sing his glories with love and devotion, Nanak(Guru says). -6-

By singing God's praises, the filth of sins are washed away.
The poison of pride which engulfs you, will disappear.
You will become free from anxiety and live in peace.
Remember God with every breath.
O mind, leave all worldly attachments.
You will attain True wealth in the association of the saints.
Gather the capital of God's Name and continue doing it.
You will obtain peace and comfort here, and respect and glory in the next world.
See One God present in all;
Only those fortunate ones can, on whose forehead such good destiny is written, Nanak(Guru says). -7-

Praise and repeat the Name of the One God.
Remember the One God and yearn for him in your mind.
Sing the glories of the One infinite God.
Repeat the Name of the One God with your mind and body.
God is the only One.
The perfect God pervades all.
All creations expanded from One God.
By worshipping One God, sins are eradicated.
The devotee, whose soul and body are imbued with God's love;
Realizes the One God with the grace of the Guru, Nanak(Guru says).
-8- (19)

Salok 20
After wandering for countless lifetimes,

I have come to seek your sanctuary.
O God, this is the humble request of Nanak(Guru says), kindly attach me to your worship.

Astpadi(Verse) 20

I, the beggar, beg you for a gift, O Lord.
Have mercy and grant me Your Name;
I beg for the dust if the saint's feet;
O Supreme Being, please fulfill my desires.
I may forever sing your praises,
I may meditate on you with every breath.
May my mind get attached to your lotus feet;
May I forever serve you.
You are my only shelter and support;
Nanak(Guru), craves for your divine Name. -1-

Supreme joy comes with the favorable glance of God.
Rare are those who taste the Nectarine Name.
Those who taste it, are satiated.
Such perfect ones never worry or lose faith.
They are filled to the brim with joy and love for God.
The yearning to meet God arises in the company if saints.
They forsake everything else and take shelter in God.
Divine Light dawns on them and they meditate on The Name, day and night.
Very fortunate ones get to repeat the Name of God.
Nanak(Guru says), real comfort is obtained through the love and devotion of the Name. -2-

The wishes of the devotee are fulfilled;
When he obtains the pure teachings of the Guru.
God is kind to His devotees,
And makes the devotee happy.
The devotee gets emancipation after his bonds with Maya(mammon) are cut.
His duality and the constant pain of births and deaths come to an end.
His desires are fulfilled and his faith bears fruit;

He is merged with God, Who is ever present with him.
God, to Whom he belongs, has merged the devotee with Himself.
He is absorbed in the service and worship of God, Nanak(Guru says). -3-

Why forget Him, Who does not let the efforts of His devotees go fruitless?
Why forget Him, Who recognizes the deeds if His devotees?
Why forget Him, Who gave us everything?
Why forget Him, Who gives life to all beings?
Why forget Him, Who protected you in the fire of the womb?
Rare are the ones who understand this, by the grace of the Guru.
Why forget Him, Who protects us from the poison of sins?
And breaks the chain of separation(from God) of countless births?
The perfect Guru has caused the devotees to understand this reality;
And they forever meditate on God, Nanak(Guru says). -4-

O true saints, do this deed;
Leave all pursuits and repeat the Name of God.
Remember, Remember, Remember the Name and get happiness.
Repeat if yourself and encourage others to do so.
Through devotion and faith in God, one swims across the world ocean.
Without sincere worship, the body is useless.
God's Name is the source if good fortune and happiness.
The drowning mortal obtains support from the Name.
All pains and troubles will vanish,
Repeat the Name, which is the treasure if virtues, Nanak(Guru says). -5-

In one(the devotee), who love, devotion and yearning for God arises;
His mind and body contain the yearning for the Name.
He attains true happiness by beholding(the Guru) with his eyes;
His mind blossoms by washing the Guru's feet.
The mind and body of the saints are imbued with the love for God.
Some rare and fortunate ones get their association.
O God! Kindly grant one thing;
That we may repeat the Name, with the grace of the Guru.
The glory of God cannot be described;

He is contained in all, Nanak(Guru says). -6-

God is the pardoner and kind to all.
He is affectionate to His devotees, and is merciful.
He is the protector of the helpless and sustainer of the world.
He is the provider of all creatures.
He is the Primal Being, who created this creation.
He is the support for the souls of the saints.
Whoever devotes his mind and repeats the Name with affection,
become sanctified.
We are virtue less, lowly and ignorant.
We seek your protection, O Supreme One, Nanak(Guru says). -7-

Salvation and deliverance can be obtained,
If one sincerely sings God's praises even for a moment.
All glory, status and kingdoms can be obtained,
For the one in whose heart the love for the Divine Name develops.
If one has relished delicious foods,
valuable attires and melodious music;
It is through the constant repetition of the Divine Name.
He is wealthy, virtuous and honorable in the true sense, I
In whose heart dwells the sermons of the Perfect Guru.
O Lord, whoever you bless to have association with the saints,
Acquires all comfort, Nanak(Guru says). -8- (20)

Salok 21
**The Formless One possesses all the three qualities of Maya,
Yet he is above them, always absorbed in profound
contemplation.
He has created all creation and remembers Himself(while seated
in all beings).**

Astpadi(Verse) 21

When the world did not exist and there was only void;
Who could commit sins or perform good deeds?
When He(God) was in profound contemplation;

With whom could anyone be hostile or unfriendly?
When there was no creation or sign of His existence;
Who could experience joy or grief?
When there existed only the Supreme Being by Himself,
Where was worldly love or attachment?
God has Himself created the world drama.
There is no other Doer, Nanak(Guru says). -1-

When only God existed by Himself;
Tell, who could be considered as liberated or entangled?
When there was only One Inaccessible and Boundless God,
Tell, who was destined to go to hell or heaven?
When God was without attributes and was in profound
contemplation;
Tell, where was soul and mammon?
When God Himself beheld His own Light;
Then who was fearful and who was fearless?
God is Himself the performer of His plays.
Nanak(Guru says), The Lord is Inaccessible and Boundless. -2-

When the Imperishable One was seated by Himself on His own
throne;
Tell, where existed birth, death and destruction?
When there was only One God, the perfect Creator;
Tell, who could be afraid of death?
When there existed only the Invisible and Inaccessible God;
Tell, who could be held accountable to the Angels of Death?
When there was only The Incomprehensible and Unfathomable
Lord,
Tell, who was free from or bound with worldly entanglements?
God, without any equal, is Himself perfect.
He Himself created His own form, Nanak(Guru says). -3-

When there existed only the Pure Supreme By Himself,
Where then was the filth of sins, and what was there to be washed?
When there existed only the Pure, Formless, Undisturbed One;
Then who was there to have feelings of pride or disgrace?
When only the Supreme Lord prevailed,
Then who could commit fraud or deceit?
When God's Light was contained within Himself;

Who could feel hunger or be satiated?
The Creator is Himself the Doer of everything and causes others to do.
Nanak(Guru says), no one can estimate God's extent. -4-

When God's glory was contained in Himself;
Where then existed mother, father, friend, son or brother?
When all powers, knowledge and accomplishments were kept with the Supreme Lord Himself;
Where then existed the holy scriptures and its readers?
When God's attributes were within His own self,
Who was there to think of good and bad omens?
When God Himself was the Highest,
Tell, who was Lord and who was Slave?
O God, your creation is magnificent and wonderful! Nanak(Guru says),
You alone know Your state and extent. -5-

When the Unperceivable, Impenetrable and Inscrutable One was by Himself,
Who was there to be influenced by mammon?
When God offered obeisance to Himself;
The three qualities of Maya could not effect anyone.
When One God alone prevailed,
Who was there to feel anxious or peaceful?
When God Himself was content with His state,
Who was there to speak and listen?
God is Boundless and the Highest of the High.
Nanak(Guru says), He alone can reach Himself. -6-

When God manifested the creation;
And spread the three qualities in it;
Then started the talk of sins and virtues;
Some suffered hell while others experienced heaven.
Then arose the snares and entanglements of mammon;
Along with ego, attachment, love, duality fear;
And pain and comfort, honor and disgrace;
And talk of different kinds started.
God Himself performs His play and Himself sees it,
When He absorbs the play of creation back into Himself,

Then He alone remains, Nanak(Guru says). -7-

Though God Himself is Invisible,
He manifests in His Saint.
God created the universe to glorify the Saint.
God Himself is the Arbiter of invisibility and manifestation.
The glory of God and His saint are known to themselves.
He Himself performs the plays, amusements and frolics.
He Himself enjoys the pleasures,
While at the same time being separated and detached from them.
He attaches to His Name, whoever He wishes to.
He causes whoever He desires, to play the worldly dramas.
O Incalculable, Unfathomable, Unaccountable, Immeasurable Lord,
As You cause Your servant Nanak(Guru), to speak, so he speaks
accordingly. -8- (21)

Salok 22
O Lord of all living beings;
You are the life force everywhere.
The One God pervades all, and none other can be seen,
Nanak(Guru says).

Astpadi(Verse) 22
He Himself speaks and hears.
He is One, yet He is All.
When it pleases Him, He creates the world.
When He wills, He absorbs it back into Himself.
Without You(God), there is nothing.
You hold the whole world on Your string.
He, upon whom God bestows understanding,
Is blessed with the True Name.
He(devotee), who looks on all men with an equal eye, realizes this
Reality!
He conquers the entire universe, Nanak(Guru says). -1-

All the creation and living beings are under His control;
He is kind to the poor, and is the patron of the helpless.
No one can destroy the person who God preserves.
He, who forgets God, is virtually dead.

Leaving Him(God), where can one go or get shelter?
One God, immune from Maya, is above all.
He(God), in whose hands are all beings,
Is with you here, there and everywhere.
The glorious God is without end, and is limitless.
His servant Nanak(Guru), is forever a sacrifice to Him. -2-

God, the Merciful One, is pervading everywhere.
He is Merciful to All.
He knows His own ways. He is present everywhere.
He cherishes the living beings in different ways;
Whatever beings were created, meditate upon Him.
Whoever is pleasing to Him, is united with Him.
Such devotees worship Him and sing His praises.
He, who in his mind, firmly believes in God;
Realizes the One God, Nanak(Guru says). -3-

He, who is attached to the Name of the One God;
His hopes shall not go in vain.
It encourages the devotee to render service;
By obeying the Divine Command, the supreme status is obtained.
There is nothing better than remembering Him;
For those in whose heart God resides.
Their attachments are broken and they become free from enmity.
They worship God's day and night.
They get comfort in this world and supreme joy in the next.
God unites them with Himself, Nanak(Guru says). -4-

Get spiritual joy in the company of saints.
Sing the praises of God, the source of joy.
Meditate and ponder on the Name and It's essence;
And get rid of duality.
Sing the sweet words of God's praises;
This is the way to save your soul from transmigration.
See God present everywhere all day and night.
This way, ignorance and darkness is dispelled.
Hear and cherish in your heart the Divine instructions.
Then you will obtain the fulfillment of your heart's desires,
Nanak(Guru says). -5-

Glorify both this life and future ones;
By cherishing the Name of God in your heart.
The perfect Guru's teachings are perfect.
He in whose heart these(teachings) reside, realizes the Truth.
Repeat God's Name with heart, body and mind.
In doing so, grief, pain and fear will depart.
O trader, carry on the trade of the truth.
Your merchandise(Name of God), shall be of value in the next world.
Take only the support of God in your Heart.
Then you will not suffer transmigration, Nanak(Guru says). -6-

Who can go away from God?
Man is saved by meditating on the Preserver of all.
Uttering the Name if the Fearless One, all fears will vanish.
Man will get liberation by God's mercy.
He, who God protects, does not suffer pain.
By repeating the Name, his mind gets joy.
His anxiety vanishes and his pride eradicated;
None can equal such a devotee.
His interests and needs are monitored by the Guru,
And his affairs are accomplished, Guru(Nanak says). -7-

He(Guru) whose wisdom is superb and glance merciful,
By whose mere glimpse, the entire humanity is saved;
Whose lotus feet is unique, Whose glimpse is blissful and whose form is radiant;
Blessed is the devotee and one who serves Him.
He is the Omniscient Supreme Being.
Blessed is he, in whose heart such a One resides.
Death cannot effect(bother) him.
They become immortal and attain immortality(freedom from transmigration);
Those who have meditated upon God,
In the holy company of the Guru, Nanak(Guru says). -8- (22)

Salok 23
On whom the Guru provides divine knowledge,
His darkness and ignorance is eradicated.

Whoever meets the Saint by God's grace,
Divine Light shines in his mind, Nanak(Guru says).

Astpadi(Verse) 23

God is realized in the holy association of the saints;
Them, the Divine Name tastes sweet.
From the One God only,
All visible things of various colors and forms emerge.
The true wealth, beyond the nine treasures, is God's Name.
It dwells within one's self.
Within, is deep meditation along with the spontaneous flow of
divine music.
This wondrous ecstasy is beyond description.
Only they can see(experience it), to whom God Himself shows.
True perception is granted to Him, Nanak(Guru says). -1-

The Boundless One exists within us as well as outside.
God pervades in every heart.
He is present on earth, heaven and all the nether regions.
He is the sustainer if all regions.
In forests, on blades if grass and mountains is present the Supreme
Being.
As He Commands, so dies his creation act.
In wind, water and fire,
And in all four quarters and ten directions, He is contained.
There is no place devoid of His presence.
By the Guru's grace, divine happiness is obtained, Nanak(Guru
says). -2-

This presence manifests on all creation and holy scriptures;
God alone is present in the moon, sun and stars.
In fact, it is the language of God that all beings speak.
He is steady and never wavers.
Through His power, He stages the world drama.
His attributes are priceless and their worth cannot be assessed.
His light shines in all; And he supports all.
Those, who have destroyed the illusion of Maya by the grace of the
Guru;
They develop firm faith in God, Nanak(Guru says). -3-

The saints see God manifested in everything;
The hearts of saints embrace the essence of all religion;
The saints listen only to divine hymns;
The saints remain absorbed in the all pervading God.
The realized saint develops the way of life;
That he utters Truth and only Truth.
Whatever happens, he accepts with bliss;
For he knows that God is the cause and effect of everything.
God lives within all and outside too;
Behold him in everything, Nanak(Guru says). -4-

God is the embodiment of Truth,
And whatever He has created is all Truth.
The entire creation is through God alone.
When he wishes, He expands and creates from Himself;
When he wishes, He absorbs all and becomes One again.
Countless are his powers and one can't comprehend His status;
Whoever He wishes, gets united with Him.
Who can be classified as close to Him, or away from Him?
When He Himself pervades All.
The one, who realizes God within his own self;
To Him, God grants consciousness of His Omnipresence,
Nanak(Guru says). -5-

God Himself functions in all beings;
He Himself is the Light in all beings.
The entire creation is His body;
He Himself performs His praises and hears them too.
He has created this theatre in which life and death is simply a play.
He has created Maya(Mammon) as His obedient functionary.
He lives in all and yet remains detached from all.
He speaks through his creation what he wants.
Everything comes and goes by His Will;
When He wills, He merges everything into His Own Self,
Nanak(Guru says). -6-

Whatever happens by His Will cannot be considered as bad;
Tell, who else is capable of doing anything?
He Himself is good and benevolent;

He Himself knows his own state.
He Himself is True, and whatever He sustains, is also truth.
He has blended Himself with His creation.
His condition and limits cannot be described in words;
It would be possible only by one that is like Him.
All His doings must be acceptable;
Such an understanding can be imparted by the grace of a Guru,
Nanak(Guru says). -7-

Whoever realizes Him, remains in comfort and peace;
God Himself unites the one with Himself;
He, in whose heart God resides, is considered to be wealthy,
honorable and blessed. Blessed, Blessed, Blessed is such a person;
By whose grace the whole world is saved.
The purpose of coming of such a blessed man is,
That in his company the yearning for the Name(of God) arises.
He saves Himself and also the world.
Ever bow to such a person, Nanak(Guru says). -8- (23)

Salok 24

He who remembers the Perfect God and His Perfect Name;
Attains union with the Perfect One.
Sing the praise of the Perfect One, Nanak(Guru says).

Astpadi(Verse) 24

Hear the sermons of the Perfect Guru;
And see the Supreme Lord nearby.
Remember God with every breath.
And the worries of the mind will depart.
Abandon the desires for the perishable things;
O mind, pray for the dust of feet it saints(blessings).
Abandon Ego and pray for his mercy;
Swim across the ocean of fire(transmigration) in the company of saints.
Fill yourself with the wealth of God's Name.
Bow before the pure Guru, Nanak(Guru says). -1-

Happiness, comfort, spiritual peace and joy are present(within);
Repeat God's Name in the company of saints.
Save your soul from the fires of hell;
Drink the nectarine essence of the Name of God.
Meditate solely upon God in your mind;
Who has One Form but many manifestations.
He is the Sustainer, the Holder of Maya, and Compassionate.
He is Merciful and is the Destroyer of miseries.
Remember(Repeat) the Name over and over again.
This is the only Sustainer of the soul, Nanak(Guru says). -2-

The words of the Guru are the holiest hymns.
They are like priceless gems.
Whoever listens and acts upon them, are saved.
He Himself is liberated and causes other to do so.
Blessed is the life and blessed is the company of the devotee;
Whose mind is imbued with God's love.
Within him, the Divine Melody plays, hailing his victory over
Maya(mammon).
Hearing it he gets Divine Joy and hails God.
His radiates from the forehead of such a saint.
Many people are saved in his company, Nanak(Guru says). -3-

Having learnt that He is capable of granting refuge, we come to Him.
By His grace He united is with Him.
Our hatred has vanished, and we have become the foot-dust(humble)
of all.
This change comes through uttering the nectarine Name in the
company of saints.
The Guru is now pleased with his devotees.
The service of the devotees is now complete.
Freed from the entanglements of the world and sins;
We now hear the Name and repeat it with our tongue.
God has so kindly extended His compassion to us.
Our cargo(of God's worship) has been accepted, Nanak(Guru says)
- 4 -

Praise God, O my saint friend;
With full attention and a concentrated mind.

The Sukhmani is in equilibrium, giving the Name of God and His attributes.
He, in whose heart it dwells, shall become the embodiment of divine virtues.
All his desires are fulfilled;
And he becomes a distinguished person, renowned throughout the world.
He achieves the highest status.
He no longer suffers transmigration.
He leaves this world with the well earned wealth of the Name;
Only he, who has obtained this gift, Nanak(Guru says). -5-

Eternal joy and peace, hidden powers, and the nine treasures;
Divine knowledge, wisdom and all spiritual powers;
Learning and intense service, meditating on God and union with Him;
Divine wisdom and the most purifying baths;
All the four blessings, and the perfect enlightenment of the soul;
Immunity from temptation while living in the world;
Beauty, Divine Intelligence and knowledge of the reality;
The capability of looking on all men as equal,
And the realization of the One in everything;
All the above mentioned blessings are bestowed upon one,
Who recites God's Name;
And with a concentrated mind,
Hears the *Name-Word* of the Guru, Nanak(Guru says). -6-

The Divine Name is a treasure and whoever utters it in his mind;
Is saved in all ages.
The praises of God and constant uttering of the Divine Name and Guru's teachings,
Is in fact discovering the essence of the Holy Scriptures.
God's Name alone is the gist of the teachings of all religion.
The Name dwells in the heart of God's saints.
Millions of sins are erased in the company of the Guru.
With the grace of the Guru, man is saved from the messenger of death.
They, on whose forehead such a destiny is written by God;
Seek the protection of Guru, Nanak(Guru says). -7-

He in whose heart the Name resides, or who listens to it with devotion;
Such one ever remembers God on his mind;
The pains of births and deaths(transmigration) is removed.
The rare human life fulfills it's true purpose of removing duality, and is saved.
He earns true fame, and nectar(divine teachings) flows from him.
His mind is absorbed only with God's Name.
Grief, disease and duality, all these vanish.
He is called a Saint and his deeds are virtuous.
His fame shall be the most exalted of all.
Nanak(Guru says), this quality, is Named Sukhmani(Jewel of Peace). -8- (24)

Complete.

Read the Divine Sukhmani over and over as often as you can, and peace will come to your life, through the remembrance of the Lord. May you be Happy; May everybody and everything be Happy.

God Bless All!

Made in the USA
Middletown, DE
08 January 2020